Comprehensive Car Buying Guide

Copyright © 2017 by Travis Johnson. All Rights Reserved.

No part of this publication may be reproduced, stored in a retrieval system or transmitted in any way by any means, electronic, mechanical, photocopy, recording or otherwise without the prior permission of the author except as provided by USA copyright law.

Published by CLC Publishing, LLC.

This novel is a work of fiction. Names, descriptions, entities, and incidents included in the story are products of the author's imagination. Any resemblance to actual persons, events, and entities is entirely coincidental.

Published in the United States of America

ISBN: 978-1985239067

COMPREHENSIVE CAR BUYING GUIDE

STEP BY STEP GUIDE: SAVE UP TO $30,000 ON YOUR NEXT CAR!

Presented by: No Name Financial

"It's not about us, it's about you."

Contents

Decide on the Right Vehicle for You 10

Shop Around 13

Secure Financing 18

Talk to the Dealer 21

Test Drive the Vehicle 24

Finalize the Financing 28

Get the Most for Your Trade-In 31

CONGRATULATIONS! 33

In today's market most of our shopping, or at least research, is done online. Car buying is no different. With sites such as Edmunds, CarGurus, CarMax, TexasAutoOnline, and Carvana it's no wonder that online has become the preferred method. In fact if you've already decided on the vehicle that fits your needs you have likely already spent time comparison shopping on some of these sites. If you walk onto a dealership without doing your research or knowing some of their tactics you may just leave with a car you didn't plan on buying. Don't worry, the salesman will tell you about buyer's remorse to try and ease your pain when you come to your senses in a few days. These highly trained salesmen are hoping that you're unprepared and will walk away with the best deal for them and not for you.

I'm not a fan of debt that doesn't build wealth or allow you to earn extra income, but I know that buying a car for cash isn't always in the cards; especially if you're just starting out. I also know that buying and even financing a vehicle is no easy task. Together we will walk through these 7 simple steps.

Decide on the Right Vehicle for You

If you plan on purchasing a vehicle for your family this is will likely take some time to answer. A few questions to consider would be: Is my family done growing? Is there room for your pets to travel? Do your golf clubs fit in the truck? Are you actually going to use a truck without a business that requires it? Are you better off repairing your current vehicle instead of replacing it? Not spending the appropriate amount of time on this step will hurt your chances of getting the right car for your needs. Be sure to consult your insurance agent for minimum insurance coverage required for your new ride. If you are switching from liability know that financed vehicles require full coverage and there are many options that fall into the range of full coverage.

A friend of mine was making decent money and was pretty sure his family of three was set in stone. At first he set out to look for his next car. A two seat muscle car was right up his alley. He found that model he wanted, at a steal of a price, had most of the extras he wanted, but something wasn't quite right. But he was becoming more responsible and the muscle car no longer fit his character and technically couldn't fit his kid in the backseat safely. He decided not to buy that car even though he wanted it and could afford it. A few weeks later they discovered his wife was pregnant with their second child. And now he set out to find the vehicle that would truly fit their changing circumstances. Had he bought the muscle car when he originally decided, he would have needed to sell it and certainly taken a loss on the deal but he was rewarded by not buying impulsively. Buying for need always trumps buying for want.

Shop Around

Once you've decided on the vehicle it's time to start shopping around. I love CarGurus for its refined search capabilities. CarGurus is used by dealerships and private parties to list their vehicles and is a great tool to not only compare prices but also to find the vehicle you're looking for in a place you would not normally look. I also use TexasAutoOnline and CarMax to compare prices on great vehicles with reasonable prices. CarMax will even give you a written offer to buy your trade-in good for 7 days whether you buy from them or not. To get the best offer from CarMax make sure to use some elbow grease and get your car looking immaculate before you bring it in. The cleanliness of your trade-in will affect their offer by as much as 20% but more on the trade-in in a moment.

New cars have horribly inflated prices. Trustedchoice.com states on average a new car will lose 19% of its value once driven off the lot. Would you invest with a company that guaranteed a 19% loss the first year? Of course not, that's ridiculous. You would be outraged and fire your broker. The deal you're looking for is a vehicle 2-6 years old and less than 60,000 miles. This is where the savings live! I saved over $60,000 combined on my last two vehicle purchases by ensuring my vehicle met these year/mileage requirements. Be smart and get the most bang for your buck.

Instead of a brand new vehicle you find a 6 year old truck with 60,000 miles on it. The truck is in great shape and you work a deal for $12,000. That is massive savings compared to the $45,000 brand new. You could drive that truck for the next 10 or so years putting another 120,000 miles on it and still be able to sell it for $5,000 when it's all said and done. That $5,000 is a nice down payment for your next vehicle.

Cars today aren't built like the last generation. Everyone has been to engineering school. We use unleaded gas and synthetic oil. We have CNC machines and NTSB safety standards. Many of these cars will last 300,000 miles with proper maintenance. Buying cars for their longevity is how we get ahead with owning our own cars.

After finally deciding to sell my last vehicle, I searched for a few months and I was getting pretty disheartened. I found vehicles I liked and even test drove but something was bothering me. It was important to me that I got a good deal. After refining my research I found a 2 year old GMC Sierra with 46,000 miles for $23,000. A new Sierra would have cost me $55,000. I'm so glad I waited until finding the right deal for me.

Secure Financing

Securing the loan is a big, important step in the car buying process. Failure to secure pre-approval from your credit union or bank ahead of time will likely cost you more in the end. Many dealerships can offer financing and I'll certainly let them compete for my business. Remember, the final price ALWAYS dictates the payment. If you haggle the monthly payment as opposed to final price watch out for they may be adding years to the loan. CarMax has a fantastic payment calculator on their page at https://www.carmax.com/car-financing/car-payment-calculator.

Some dealerships may offer a rate better than your financial institution up front then call later, after you've been driving the car for a few days, to tell you they were unable to secure the loan at that rate. At this point you have a few options. You can take the new rate (which is what they want), you can use the loan that you already secured via your own financial institution, or you may simply return the vehicle. If you decide to take the new rate offered by the dealership you should know that they may be taking you for a ride. A few percentage points for you might only mean $15 each month but when the dealership does that for every car sold it can mean thousands of dollars in their

pockets each month for nothing.

Talk to the Dealer

You've decided on the car, found the right deal, and secured the loan; it's time to talk to the dealer. You can coordinate with the dealer online, over the phone, or in person. I have several friends who negotiated the entire deal via email and didn't go to the dealership until it was time to drive the car off the lot. If you decide on this route and show up to the dealership having decided everything congrats! You have successfully dodged some of the dealer's tricks of the trade. If you show up in person you must watch out for salesman playing "hide the keys" and "disappear to find the manager."

The "hide the keys" game comes into play when they are evaluating your trade in but you've decided it's time to leave. Suddenly, they can't find your keys to let you go. This is usually when they send in their bulldog to try a high pressure close on you consisting of pressure and guilt. You can avoid this by bringing your spare set of keys or simply walking into the manager's office to take your keys back. The "disappear to find the manager" game happens when you've taken a hard line on a price and you send them to go negotiate. Most times they stick their head in the office with the manager to tell them they are going to go smoke and leave you sitting in their office waiting for an answer to a question they may never ask. You can avoid this by asking your sales associate up front if he has the power to approve any negotiations. If they don't have that authority simply ask to only deal with someone who has that authority.

Of course there are a few ways to avoid these games all together. Using CarMax or a similar company that offers no-haggle pricing on every vehicle or by using Carvana where the entire experience is 100% online and they deliver the car to your door. Many deliveries are free of charge.

Test Drive the Vehicle

The test drive and personal inspection is one of the most important steps to the car buying experience. In fact once you've decided on the car for you it's highly recommend test driving the car at another dealership before driving at the dealership of your choice. In a pinch you could rent one for a day or two but a free test drive is preferred. Conduct your test drive at another dealership so you can really check out that car without any pressure to buy. You must know that without a doubt that you will not be buying that car on that test drive, all the interactions with the sales associate are streamlined and carefree. Ensure you check blind spots, comfort, and most importantly see if you actually like to drive it before you get to the place where you expect to drive it off the lot. Once the pre-test drive is complete you have something to compare your real test drive to in the future.

Don't be afraid to ask for an extended test drive. Last summer I asked for a four day test drive on a 2015 Green Flash special edition Camaro. I told them I could pay cash for the vehicle but that I had back problems. I would hate to buy a $45,000 car and discover after a week of driving that the car was hurting my back. They agreed and I got to drive that magical car over the long weekend. Low and behold that although the Camaro was an amazing car to drive, it did in fact hurt my back. I returned the car on Monday to a disappointed salesman but they upheld our agreement. Ask for that long test drive. Go buy groceries and install that car seat. Have friends in the back to let you know how comfortable the ride is. Be prepared to give the car back if it's not exactly what you want.

During the walk around make sure to check the tires for tread wear and rot. Inspect all the glass for chips and the seals for cracks. Open the hood and check fluid levels, smell the fluids, and check for anything that doesn't appear to belong. Make sure you have the sales associate explain all features you're unfamiliar with before driving off the lot. If you have any questions about the walk around have it checked by a mechanic you trust. The extra time spent here will save hassle later.

Finalize the Financing

Congrats! You've decided you buy the car but you still have to talk to the finance person to finalize the paperwork. Don't be lulled into a false sense of security. The finance guy makes just as much if not more than the sales associate you've been dealing with all day. They will offer you add-ons such as under coating, premium wheels, an extra warranty, oil changes, a maintenance package, nitrogen in your tires, and gap insurance. This is the time to let them know you have secured your own financing but are willing to let them compete for your business. When they know you have an ace in the whole they are less likely to try and pull the bait-and-switch on financing.

Make sure they know you refuse to finance anything over 60 months. Any loan longer than this and will assuredly be upside down on your loan the entire time you own the vehicle. That lower payment may look more attractive but will always end up costing you more in the end. Of all the add-ons they offer the only one I ever consider is gap insurance. Gap insurance will ensure your car loan gets paid off completely in the event you total your car before it's paid off. Keep in mind this price is negotiable and often offered through your own insurance company. If you've bought a car in the year range I've indicated then your car will likely still having some warranty remaining even though you are not the original buyer. Everything else offered by the finance department isn't likely worth your time. Be wary of hidden fees so you aren't blindsided. If unprepared for the extra expense your new loan might break your budget.

Get the Most for Your Trade-In

Now that everything has been agreed upon it's time to talk trade-in and down payment. You should know the market price for your ride (check CarGurus, NADA etc.) and already have a deal to sell it outright to CarMax. If you tell the dealership about the trade-in too early they will use the projected figures based on the secondary sale of your trade-in. It is NOT recommended that you roll any negative equity into your new loan. Doing this means you will never get ahead. They only way to truly get value out of your personal vehicle is by paying it off and driving it for several years while saving for your next one. Shady dealerships always have seemingly fantastic deals if you have negative equity but only on the latest model. Remember that instant 19% plummet in value, don't let that be you.

CONGRATULATIONS!

Congratulations on buying your new ride! The car buying experience can be tricky and a headache if you're uninformed. By applying these lessons you successfully saved thousands of dollars and can brag to your friends about the great deal you got. Without a doubt you must remember that you hold all the power in this negotiation. If at any time the deal doesn't look, feel, or smell right you MUST walk away. Regardless of what they tell you there is always another car and always another deal.

www.ingramcontent.com/pod-product-compliance
Lightning Source LLC
Chambersburg PA
CBHW030105230526
45471CB00003B/1260